HANGOVER
═FOOD═

FOR WHEN YOU'RE
hurting AND
hungry

restorative
35
recipes

DOG 'n' BONE

Published in 2019 by Dog 'n' Bone Books
An imprint of Ryland Peters & Small Ltd
20–21 Jockey's Fields   341 E 116th St
London WC1R 4BW   New York, NY 10029

www.rylandpeters.com

10 9 8 7 6 5 4 3 2 1

Text © Susannah Blake, Ross Dobson, Amy Ruth
Finegold, Felipe Fuentes Cruz & Ben Fordham,
Dunja Gulin, Carol Hilker, Dan May, Hannah Miles,
Shelagh Ryan, Sonia Stevenson, Leah Vanderveldt,
Sunil Vijayakar, and Dog 'n' Bone Books 2019
Design and photography © Dog 'n' Bone Books
2019

A CIP catalog record for this book is available from
the Library of Congress and the British Library.

ISBN: 978 1 912983 03 2

Printed in China

Designer: Emily Breen
Recipe credits: See page 64
Photography credits: Martin Brigdale 63; Peter
Cassidy 1, 5–9, 13, 21–34; Adrian Lawrence 14;
William Lingwood 11; Steve Painter 57; William
Reavell 18, 58; Toby Scott 3, 39, 44; Kate
Whitaker 2, 17, 43, 47; Clare Winfield 37,
48–55, 61
Illustrations: Emrah Avci/Dreamstime.com

CONTENTS

1 BACON AND EGGS

2 SANDWICHES

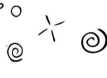

3 COMFORT FOOD

4 SWEETNESS

HUEVOS RANCHEROS

This dish is hot, which makes it a great hangover cure, particularly when served with a large hair-of-the-dog Bloody Mary. If you prefer it slightly milder, just reduce the amount of fiery green chili appropriately. Top it all off with a tomato salsa and enjoy, ideally sat outside in the sunshine wearing very dark sunglasses!

½ tablespoon olive oil

8 slices bacon, finely chopped

1 large onion, finely chopped

1 garlic clove, crushed

4 hot green chilis, finely chopped

1 mild red chili, deseeded and finely chopped

4 tomatoes, skinned and roughly chopped

½ teaspoon sea salt

¼ teaspoon freshly ground black pepper

8 eggs

4 plain 8-in./20-cm flour tortillas

Tomato salsa, to serve

SERVES 4

Heat the oil in a skillet/frying pan and gently fry the bacon until almost cooked. Drain off all but 1 teaspoon of the fat.

Add the onion and garlic to the pan and cook, allowing to brown lightly. Add the chilis, tomatoes, salt, and pepper, stir well, and cover. Bring to a boil, reduce the heat, and simmer for about 20 minutes, stirring frequently.

Meanwhile, fry or poach the eggs to your taste and gently warm the tortillas in a skillet or warm oven.

To serve, place 2 eggs per person on a warmed tortilla and liberally spoon the salsa over the eggs. Eat immediately!

HAM AND EGGS TACOS

Most Mexican households start their day with a breakfast of eggs, so this dish makes sense if you're suffering the consequences of too many tequilas. There are endless flavor combinations in Mexican cuisine, but let's keep things simple by combining creamy eggs and salty ham with a zesty salsa that provides a little balance when you might be struggling to keep yours. Salsa verde works well here—its gentle vibrancy should bring your taste buds back to life—but any salsa will do the job. You can pick your favorite or just go with whatever is lurking at the back of the fridge. Don't forget to add the cheese at the end—you owe it to yourself!

6 eggs

1 tablespoon salsa (ideally salsa verde)

2 tablespoons vegetable oil

4½ oz./125g (6–8 thin slices) ham, chopped into pieces

1 teaspoon salt

SERVE WITH

8–12 flour or corn tortillas, warmed

Salsa (ideally salsa verde)

1 cup/100g grated cheese (ideally Monterey Jack or mild Cheddar)

SERVES 3–4

Break the eggs into a bowl, add the salsa, and whisk for about 30 seconds.

Heat the oil in a saucepan over a low-medium heat, then add the chopped ham and salt, and sauté for a few seconds. Add the beaten eggs and cook for about 1–2 minutes, stirring gently.

While the eggs are cooking, gently heat the tortillas in a skillet/frying pan or warm oven. Place the warmed tortillas on the table together with the ham and eggs, a bowl of salsa, and the grated cheese, and let everyone help themselves.

STEAK AND EGG SKILLET

Here's a new take on traditional steak and eggs. Fry, scramble, or poach the eggs—there are many ways to give this your own twist!

3 tablespoons olive oil

1 onion, chopped

2 carrots, chopped

3 sticks celery, chopped

1 garlic clove, halved

3 tablespoons tomato paste/purée

1 cup/250 ml red wine

1¾ quarts/2 liters chicken stock

4 tablespoons brown sugar

⅓ cup/80 ml Worcestershire sauce

2 tablespoons soy sauce

Handful of fresh thyme

3 fresh bay leaves

4–5 beef thin/short rib(s), boneless, uncooked

Sea salt and freshly ground black pepper

FOR THE HASH

½ cup/120 g potatoes, diced

Butter, for frying

1 tablespoon olive oil

½ onion, diced

1 shallot, minced

2 garlic cloves, minced

A few sprigs of fresh thyme

A few sprigs of flat-leaf parsley, chopped

Sea salt and freshly ground black pepper

SERVE WITH

4 fried eggs

Hollandaise sauce (see page 10)

Oven-safe skillet/ frying pan

SERVES 4

Preheat the oven to 300°F/150°C/Gas 2.

Add the olive oil to an oven-safe skillet/ frying pan and over a medium heat caramelize the onion, carrots, celery, and garlic. Add the tomato paste/purée and cook for 1–2 minutes. Add the red wine and reduce the mixture by half. Add the stock, brown sugar, Worcestershire sauce, soy sauce, thyme, and bay leaves. Season generously with salt and pepper, and boil. Add the thin/short rib(s) and transfer the pan to the preheated oven for 2 hours or until the meat is tender. Remove the pan from the oven, strain and reserve the liquid, and discard the vegetables and herbs. Over a medium heat, boil the reserved liquid to skim off the fat and reduce until it coats the back of a spoon. Set this braising liquid aside while you make the hash.

For the hash, fill a saucepan with water and bring to a boil. Blanch the potatoes until they are tender. Drain the potatoes and run under cold water to stop them from cooking. Heat the butter in a skillet, add the potatoes, and fry until lightly brown. Set aside. Add the olive oil to the skillet and caramelize the onion over a medium heat. Add the shallot and garlic and continue cooking until the mixture is golden.

Dice the thin/short rib(s) and add to the pan of potatoes, onion, shallot, and garlic. Add the reserved braising liquid to moisten and mix in the thyme and parsley. Season with salt and pepper. Serve with a fried egg on top and with Hollandaise sauce on the side.

PARIS-STYLE EGGS BENEDICT

Delicious bacon, gooey cheese, perfectly oozing poached eggs... This twist on a traditional French breakfast already sounds like the Holy Trinity of morning-after munch. Throw in a buttery croissant and drizzle with homemade Hollandaise sauce and you've basically died and gone to hangover food heaven. Eating this dish is an almost religious experience, just perfect for a Sunday serving.

¼ cup/60 g butter

4 slices bacon

2 teaspoons vinegar (preferably distilled)

4 eggs

4 croissants

Butter, for spreading

8 slices Brie cheese

A dash of Tabasco sauce (optional)

Freshly ground black pepper

A couple of sprigs flat-leaf parsley, chopped, to garnish

CLASSIC HOLLANDAISE

⅔ cup/140 g unsalted butter

3 egg yolks

1 tablespoon fresh lemon juice

½ teaspoon salt

SERVES 4

To make the Hollandaise sauce, melt the butter in a small saucepan. Put the egg yolks, lemon juice, and salt in a blender and blend on medium to medium-high speed for 25 seconds or until the eggs lighten in color. Change the blender speed to the lowest setting and, very slowly, pour in the hot butter and continue to blend. Add more salt and lemon juice to taste. Transfer to a small pitcher/jug.

Melt some butter in a large skillet/frying pan over a low to medium heat, and, when the pan is hot, add the bacon, turning it occasionally until warm.

While the bacon is cooking, fill a large saucepan with water and bring to a boil. Add the vinegar and let the water come to a boil again. After the water boils, reduce to a simmer.

Next, poach the eggs. The easiest way is to do one egg at a time. Crack the egg into a small bowl and slip it into the barely simmering water. Once the egg begins to solidify, slip in the next egg and so on until you have all 4 cooking. Turn the heat off, cover the pan with a lid, and let the eggs sit for 3–4 minutes, depending on how runny you like them. Starting with the first egg you cracked, gently lift them out with a slotted spoon and set them down in a bowl or on a plate.

Toast and butter the croissants. Top each with the bacon, 2 slices of Brie, and a poached egg. Sprinkle on Tabasco sauce if desired. Pour the Hollandaise sauce over the top, garnish with parsley, and season with ground black pepper to taste.

EGGS FLORENTINE

If you're suffering after a night on the sauce AND you're a vegetarian, then sadly the recipe to your left is not the one for you. However, don't be sad; chuck out the pork, throw some spinach on top instead, and you've got Eggs Florentine. The vegetable element here is presumably also incredibly good for your aching internal bits. Let's just ignore all that butter in the Hollandaise, eh?

2 eggs

1 tablespoon vinegar
(preferably distilled)

1 tablespoon/15 g butter,
plus extra for spreading

7 oz./200 g baby
spinach leaves

Pinch of freshly grated
nutmeg

2 English muffins

2–4 tablespoons
Hollandaise sauce
(see page 10)

Sea salt and freshly ground
black pepper

SERVES 2

To poach the eggs, bring a saucepan of lightly salted water to a boil. Add the vinegar and reduce to a gentle simmer. Swirl the water with a fork and crack the eggs one at a time into the water. Cook for 3 minutes and remove with a slotted spoon.

Meanwhile, melt the butter in a saucepan, then add the spinach. Cook for about 3 minutes, stirring occasionally, until the spinach begins to wilt. Season with nutmeg and salt and pepper to taste. Remove from the heat, cover, and keep warm.

Toast the muffins whole and spread with butter. Spoon some spinach onto each muffin (taking care to drain off any excess liquid as you do so). Set an egg on top, spoon over the Hollandaise sauce, sprinkle with a little more pepper, and serve immediately.

BELGIAN WAFFLES WITH MAPLE-CURED BACON

In recognition of the amount of gin-induced nonsense you spouted at 2am this morning, it's time to cook waffles. Yes, you really did say that to your friends, but fear not; the delightfully salty and sweet maple bacon will assuage any feelings of hangxiety you are experiencing.

3 eggs, separated

1½ cups/360 ml buttermilk

1 stick/115 g unsalted butter, melted and cooled

½ teaspoon vanilla paste or extract, or ½ a vanilla pod/bean

1½ cups/200 g all-purpose/plain flour

1 teaspoon baking/bicarbonate of soda

1½ teaspoons baking powder

¼ teaspoon salt

3 tablespoons granulated sugar

½ teaspoon ground cinnamon

Pre-bought, thin-cut maple-cured bacon, 1–2 slices per waffle

SERVE WITH

Softened butter or ice cream

Maple syrup

Waffle maker

SERVES 4

Measure out all the ingredients ahead of time. This will help the recipe come together quickly. You also want to make sure all the ingredients are at room temperature.

Preheat the oven to 225°F/110°C/Gas ¼ and turn on the waffle maker following the manufacturer's instructions.

In a large bowl, whisk the egg yolks. Slowly incorporate the buttermilk, butter, and vanilla. In a separate medium bowl, sift together the flour, baking/bicarbonate of soda, baking powder, salt, sugar, and cinnamon. Add the flour mixture to the egg mixture and whisk until smooth.

In another medium bowl, using a hand or free-standing mixer, whisk the egg whites until they form stiff peaks. Using a rubber spatula, fold half of the egg whites into the batter and incorporate well. After they're incorporated, fold in the remaining egg whites.

Put enough batter into the waffle maker to make a waffle and place one piece of raw bacon on top of the batter. Cook the waffle according to the manufacturer's instructions, then transfer to a baking sheet and place in the preheated oven to keep warm. Repeat the process to make each waffle.

Serve the waffles with softened butter or ice cream and some really good maple syrup.

SAUSAGE AND EGG MUFFINS

Like the Golden Arches' classic hangover buster, but hate their 10.30 curfew? Try this, you won't have to leave the house. I'm lovin' it!

4 good-quality sausages (approximately 3 oz./85 g each)

1 tablespoon olive oil

3½ oz./100 g Cheddar cheese, sliced (preferably Applewood smoked cheese)

A knob of butter, plus extra for buttering the muffins

5½ oz./150 g baby spinach

4 English muffins

4 eggs, fried, over-easy

Sea salt and freshly ground black pepper

SRIRACHA HOLLANDAISE

Hollandaise sauce (see page 10)

1 tablespoon sriracha hot sauce

Baking sheet, lined with parchment paper

SERVES 4

Start by whipping up a batch of Hollandaise using the recipe on page 10. Once the sauce is ready, stir in the sriracha sauce and season with salt to taste. Keep the Hollandaise somewhere warm with a piece of plastic wrap/clingfilm touching the surface to stop a skin forming.

Preheat the oven to 325°F/160°C/Gas 3.

Remove the casing from the sausages and shape the sausage meat filling into four flat round patties. In a skillet/frying pan, heat the olive oil over a medium heat and fry the patties on both sides until lightly browned and cooked. Place on the prepared baking sheet, top each patty with a slice of smoked cheese, and place in the preheated oven for a couple of minutes until the cheese has melted. Return the pan to the heat. Melt a knob of butter in the pan, then add the spinach and toss until it is just wilted. Season to taste with salt and pepper, and transfer to a bowl.

Slice the muffins in half horizontally and lightly toast. Butter both insides. To assemble, put the muffin bottoms on four serving plates, sit a sausage patty with the melted cheese on top of each, then some wilted spinach, then a fried egg, and spoon some Hollandaise on top. Put the other halves of the muffins on top and serve.

CHORIZO MUSHROOM EGGS

Aussies know a thing or two about boozing. Thankfully, their top café culture means they know lots about ace hangover dishes like this one.

4 eggs

Sea salt and freshly ground black pepper

Turkish bread, to serve

CHORIZO SAUCE

1 tablespoon olive oil

1 small red onion, finely chopped

2 garlic cloves, finely sliced

1 cup/120 g chorizo, cut into ¼-in./5-mm slices

14-oz./400-g can plum tomatoes

1 tablespoon balsamic vinegar

1½ teaspoons soft brown sugar

¼ teaspoon hot red pepper/dried chili flakes

½ star anise

1 x 2-in./5-cm strip orange rind, pith removed

12 basil leaves, roughly torn

BAKED MUSHROOMS

1 tablespoon/ 15 g butter

1 tablespoon olive oil

1 garlic clove, finely sliced

4 Portobello mushrooms, sliced

LEMON CRÈME FRAÎCHE

½ cup/100 g crème fraîche or soured cream

¼ teaspoon grated lemon zest

½ teaspoon fresh lemon juice

Baking sheet, greased

SERVES 4

To make the Chorizo Sauce, put the oil in a large, heavy-bottomed skillet/frying pan set over a low-medium heat and gently sauté the onion for 7–10 minutes until soft and translucent, but not colored. Add the garlic and chorizo, and cook until the chorizo starts to brown and release its oils. Add ¼ cup/60 ml of water and all the remaining ingredients except the basil. Season to taste, turn up the heat, and bring the mix to a boil. Immediately reduce the heat and simmer for 20–30 minutes, until the sauce is thick and glossy. Remove from the heat, discard the star anise and orange rind, stir in the basil, and set aside.

Preheat the oven to 350°F/180°C/Gas 4.

To prepare the mushrooms, melt the butter and olive oil in a skillet set over a medium heat. Add the sliced garlic and cook gently for 2–3 minutes, then remove the pan from the heat. Put the mushrooms on a greased baking sheet and spoon over the garlic-infused butter. Cover with foil and bake in the oven for 15–20 minutes until tender.

To make the Lemon Crème Fraîche, combine the ingredients in a bowl, cover, and set aside.

Return the Chorizo Sauce to a low heat and gently reheat. Add the Baked Mushrooms to the pan, ensuring they are evenly distributed and half submerged in the sauce. Make four holes in the sauce with a spoon and crack in the eggs. Cover and cook gently for 15–20 minutes until the whites are set and the yolks still a little runny. Season and serve with Turkish bread and the Crème Fraîche.

TOFU SCRAMBLE

Let's face it, when you have a hangover if you start to think too deeply about what an egg actually is, it's enough to turn even the strongest of stomachs. That's why vegans are onto something by using tofu to create a dish that looks and tastes very similar to scrambled eggs. Actually, way better than scrambled eggs! Asparagus is used here 'cos it's a smug superfood and ideal for reintroducing a few lost vitamins after a night on the sauce, but bung into the dish any vegetables, herbs, and spices that you fancy.

2 cups/150 g fresh shiitake mushrooms

4 tablespoons olive oil

1 cup/120 g onions sliced into thin half-moons

½ teaspoon sea salt

3 oz./85 g trimmed asparagus, sliced diagonally at the bottom

2 tablespoons tamari

½ teaspoon ground turmeric

10 oz./300 g fresh tofu, mashed with a fork

4 tablespoons water, if necessary

1 teaspoon dark sesame oil

½ teaspoon dried basil or 2 tablespoons chopped fresh basil

Freshly ground black pepper

SERVE WITH

Toasted bread

Salad (optional)

SERVES 2–3

Cut the mushrooms in half lengthwise, then into thinner wedges. Add the olive oil, onion, and salt to a wok or skillet/frying pan and sauté briefly over a medium heat, stirring energetically to prevent sticking.

Add the mushrooms, asparagus, tamari, and turmeric, and stir with two wooden spoons. When the mushrooms have soaked up a bit of tamari, turn up the heat, add the tofu, and stir for another 1–2 minutes. The scramble should be uniformly yellow in color. At this point you can add the water to make the scramble juicy, and continue cooking for a couple more minutes. However, whether you need water or not depends on how soft your tofu was to begin with—softer types are moist and don't need any water at the end of cooking.

Mix in the sesame oil and basil, season to taste with pepper, and serve warm, with a nice salad and a few slices of toasted bread.

FISH FINGER SANDWICH

The fish finger sandwich is a British hangover staple. Use any leftover lager in the batter for a richer flavor and dubious hair-of-the-dog health claims. Enjoy with a mountain of chips (or fries to non-Brits).

2 fillets of cod or haddock, skinned and boned

Sunflower or vegetable oil, for frying

French country bread

Butter, for spreading

Handful of romaine/cos lettuce leaves, cut into strips

Fries or wedges, to serve

BEER BATTER

1½ cups/200 g all-purpose/plain flour

2 teaspoons sea salt

2 x 11-fl. oz./330-ml bottles of lager

TARTARE SAUCE

1 cup/225 g mayonnaise

½ cup/80 g dill pickles

1 teaspoon capers, chopped

2 teaspoons Dijon mustard

2 teaspoons chopped shallots

2 tablespoons chopped scallions/spring onions

2 teaspoons fresh lemon juice

Tabasco sauce, to taste

Sea salt and freshly ground black pepper, to taste

SERVES 2

Prepare your fish for battering. Slice the fish into at least six finger-size strips.

For the batter, whisk the flour, salt, and lager in a bowl until combined. Fill a large skillet/frying pan with about 1 in./2.5 cm oil over a high heat, but don't leave this unattended. When the oil is bubbling steadily, it's ready to go.

Dip the fish fingers in the batter, remove any excess, and then lower carefully into the oil using tongs if necessary. Fry for about 4 minutes on each side over a moderate heat until golden and crispy.

Remove the fish fingers carefully from the oil and drain well on paper towels. Season to taste with sea salt.

Mix all the ingredients for the tartare sauce together in a mixing bowl. Cut the French country bread into thick slices. Lay one down and butter it before spreading a couple of tablespoons of tartare sauce on top. Place 3 fish fingers on top, then a few strips of lettuce, before placing a second slice of bread on top. Serve with fries or wedges.

BURGER TACOS

Putting a burger in a taco? Go back to bed chef, you're drunk! But hang on a second, cynics, what's not to like here? Tacos... good. Burgers... good... Taco burgers... logic dictates they must be good, particularly when slathered in some sensational chipotle ketchup.

1 lb. 2 oz./500 g ground/minced beef

½ yellow (bell) pepper, finely chopped

½ red (bell) pepper, finely chopped

2 garlic cloves, minced

¼ red onion, finely chopped

½ zucchini/ courgette, finely chopped

10 fresh mint leaves, finely chopped

½ teaspoon salt

½ teaspoon freshly ground black pepper

¼ teaspoon ground cumin

CHIPOTLE KETCHUP

2½ cups/600 ml tomato ketchup

1 tablespoon freshly chopped ginger

1 tablespoon chopped chipotle chili

SERVE WITH

8 slices Cheddar cheese

8 flour or corn tortillas, warmed (see page 4)

8 romaine/cos lettuce leaves

1 tomato, cut into thick slices

1 red onion, thinly sliced

SERVES 4

First make the chipotle ketchup. Place all the ingredients in a blender with 6 tablespoons water and blend for 1–2 minutes. Refrigerate until you are ready to use.

Place the ground/minced beef, peppers, garlic, onion, zucchini/courgette, mint, salt, pepper, and cumin in a mixing bowl, and mix together well.

Divide the mixture into four equal portions and form a burger with each one.

Cook the burgers in a griddle pan or skillet/ frying pan for 3–4 minutes on each side, turning occasionally to ensure the meat is cooked through. When cooked, remove from the heat, cut each burger horizontally in half, and top each with a slice of cheese.

To serve, place a tortilla on a plate, layer on a lettuce leaf, then the burger with cheese, and top with tomato and red onion. Serve with the bowl of Chipotle Ketchup for people to help themselves. Or if you wish, you can smear the ketchup over the tortillas before laying on the lettuce, burger, and other toppings.

ULTIMATE GRILLED CHEESE SANDWICH

There's no better comfort food than the grilled cheese sandwich. Easy to make and fantastically versatile, it can be as simple or as pimped up as you fancy, like this version with the obligatory bacon that your withered shell of a body demands you feed it instantly.

DIJONNAISE

2 large white onions

2 tablespoons/30 g butter

1¾ cups/400 ml light/single cream

3 tablespoons Dijon mustard

Pinch of salt, black pepper, garlic, nutmeg, chopped fresh flat-leaf parsley and tarragon

FOR THE CURED TOMATOES

2–3 tomatoes, cut into ½ in./1 cm slices

About 1 cup/250 ml olive oil

1 cup/60 g breadcrumbs, toasted

Pinch of salt

TO ASSEMBLE THE SANDWICHES

12 slices thick-cut bacon

12 slices sourdough bread, cut ½ in./ 1 cm thick

6 tablespoons/90 g salted butter, at room temperature

¼ cup/25 g Parmesan cheese, grated

1 cup/115 g Cheddar cheese, grated

1 cup/115 g Gouda cheese, grated

1 cup/115 g Provolone cheese, grated

1½ teaspoons sea salt

½ teaspoon freshly ground black pepper

Oven-safe skillet/ frying pan

MAKES 6

Make the Dijonnaise by finely chopping the onions and frying with the butter in a saucepan. Mix in the cream and mustard, season, and simmer until the sauce takes on a mustardy color and is relatively thick.

Lay the tomato slices in a pie dish and add olive oil until the slices are half-submerged. Let the tomatoes sit for 30 minutes, turning once. After that time, lift the tomatoes out of the oil and season with salt. Press them into the toasted breadcrumbs.

Preheat the oven to 325°F/160°C/Gas 3.

Fry the bacon until nicely browned. Drain the slices on paper towels, let cool, and cut into 1-in./2.5-cm pieces.

Spread 12 slices of sourdough bread lightly with butter. Flip the slices, spread with Dijonnaise, and layer the bacon on top, followed by two slices of cured tomatoes.

Mix the 4 grated cheeses in a bowl and add the salt and pepper. Pile a handful of the cheeses on top of the bacon on each sandwich. Top with the remaining bread slices, Dijonnaise side down.

Place the sandwiches in an oven-safe skillet/frying pan in the preheated oven for a few minutes so the cheese melts nicely. Remove the sandwiches from the oven and let cool for 2 minutes before serving.

PASTRAMI REUBEN

Delis undeniably make awesome hangover sandwiches, but visiting one means extracting yourself from your PJs and your festering pit of self pity. Instead, why not bring the deli delights to you? Traditionally, a Reuben sandwich is made with salt beef, but this one's been given a little pastrami makeover. Here's one for the beef fact fans (of which there aren't many): pastrami is made with beef shoulder, and salt beef is made from brisket. Fascinating.

FOR THE RUSSIAN DRESSING

1½ cups/340 g mayonnaise

⅔ cup/150 ml chili sauce

⅓ cup/75 g sour cream

2 tablespoons horseradish sauce

1 tablespoon fresh lemon juice

2 teaspoons sugar

2 teaspoons Worcestershire sauce

½ teaspoon hot sauce

½ teaspoon paprika

1 dill pickle, chopped

1 scallion/spring onion, chopped

Salt and freshly ground black pepper

TO ASSEMBLE THE SANDWICHES

1⅓ cups/225 g sauerkraut, drained and squeezed of moisture

8 slices rye bread

8–16 slices Provolone cheese

1 lb./450 g pastrami, shaved

Salted butter, softened, for spreading

Fries, to serve

Griddle pan or ridged stove-top pan

MAKES 4

To make the Russian dressing, mix all the ingredients in a food processor until combined. Season to taste with salt and pepper. Refrigerate.

Build the sandwich: mix half of the Russian dressing with the sauerkraut. Lay 4 slices of rye bread down and place 1–2 slices of Provolone cheese on each one, followed by a generous serving of pastrami and another 1–2 slices of cheese. Top with the sauerkraut mixture and a second piece of bread. Butter the outside of the sandwiches. Heat a griddle pan or a ridged stove-top pan over a low-medium heat. Add the sandwiches and grill for about 2–3 minutes per side, until the cheese has melted.

Serve with fries and extra Russian dressing on the side.

CLUB SANDWICH

Did you know, rapper 50 Cent's 2003 hit, "In Da Club," was inspired by his love of club sandwiches. No? Unsurprising really since it's a completely made-up fact. Still it's not that much of a stretch to imagine Fiddy, Dre, and Eminem chowing down on a round of club sandwiches at the end of an epic all-night studio session. What's this got to do with hangovers? Not a lot, but, with a triple threat of bacon, turkey, and ham, it's hard to argue that a club sandwich won't go a long way to fixing yours if you've been partying like it's your birthday.

12 slices sourdough bread

2 medium avocados

8 romaine/cos lettuce leaves

¾ cup/175 g mayonnaise or Dijonnaise (see page 24)

3 large tomatoes, cut into 16 thick slices

16 slices bacon

8 slices roasted turkey breast

16 slices cured ham

8 slices Fontina cheese

Sea salt and freshly ground black pepper, to taste

16 toothpicks/ cocktail sticks

MAKES 4

Toast the sourdough bread under a broiler/grill on both sides. Pit/stone, peel, and slice the avocados. Finely chop the lettuce and arrange it into 8 stacks.

Arrange 3 bread slices in a row. Spread 1 tablespoon of Dijonnaise over 1 side of each slice of bread. Place a lettuce stack on the top of the first slice of bread. Top with 2 tomato slices and a few slices of avocado, and season with salt and pepper if needed. Place 2 slices of bacon on top, then a slice of turkey, 2 slices of ham, and a slice of the Fontina cheese. Season to taste with salt and pepper. Place the second bread slice on top and repeat the layering. Cover with the third bread slice, Dijonnaise side facing down.

Pin the sandwich together by piercing it with 4 toothpicks/cocktail sticks arranged in a diamond pattern. Repeat the whole process to form another 3 sandwiches.

STEAK SANDWICH

Well done, you've managed to drag yourself out of bed, and you're heading to the pub for some comfort food. You spend the whole journey there thinking what to have. You decide on a steak sandwich and start drooling at the thought of perfectly spiced rare steak, topped with sautéed onions and blue cheese to add the right amount of flavor and texture when placed on a crispy loaf of bread. But wait, you booze-addled idiot; it's 10 in the morning and the pub doesn't open for at least two hours. You'd better head home via the supermarket and make this one instead.

2 x 12 oz./350 g New York strip/sirloin steaks, cut 1 in./2.5 cm thick

Olive oil, for frying

4 onions, sliced into rings

½ teaspoon fresh thyme leaves

2 garlic cloves, minced

1–2 crispy loaves of bread, such as French country bread or ciabatta

4 tablespoons Dijonnaise (see page 24)

1 cup/30 g arugula/rocket

4–8 oz./115–225 g blue cheese, crumbled

Sea salt and freshly ground black pepper

Fries or wedges, to serve

MAKES 4

Season the steaks to taste with salt and pepper on both sides. Heat 2–4 tablespoons of olive oil in a medium skillet/frying pan over a high heat until it's very hot, almost smoking. Sear the steaks for 1½ minutes per side and then reduce the heat to low and cook the steaks for about 3–4 minutes, turning once. Remove the steaks from the pan and place on a plate. Cover tightly with foil and sit in the refrigerator for 10 minutes. Remove and slice the steak into strips.

Using the same pan, heat 3 more tablespoons of olive oil over a medium heat. Add the onion ringts and thyme, and sauté for 10 minutes, stirring occasionally, until the onion is caramelized. Add the garlic for the last 1–2 minutes.

Cut the bread lengthwise and into large sandwich rolls. Spread 1 tablespoon of Dijonnaise on the bottom half of each roll. Place a layer of the steak strips on top of the Dijonnaise, sprinkle with salt and pepper, and top with the caramelized onion rings. Place the arugula/rocket on top of the onion rings and sprinkle a handful of blue cheese on top. Cover with the top half of the buns.

Serve with fries or wedges.

SALT BEEF HASH EGG SANDWICH

Close your eyes and think of the elements that constitute the ultimate hangover-annihilating sandwich. Does it conjure up images of oozing Swiss cheese, melt-in-the-mouth salt beef, and an egg yolk seductively dripping down the edge of a bun? Now open your eyes. Your dreams have become reality, because here's the recipe for that perfect egg sandwich.

½ stick/60 g unsalted butter, plus extra for spreading

1 tablespoon olive oil

4 eggs

4 sturdy buns

2 lb./900 g salt beef, thickly sliced

4–8 slices Swiss cheese

Sea salt and freshly ground black pepper

SERVE WITH

Yellow mustard

4 dill pickles

MAKES 4

Heat the butter in a large skillet/frying pan over a medium-high heat. Add the olive oil and, after the butter starts to bubble, crack the eggs into the pan, being careful not to break the yolks. Season to taste with salt and pepper. Fry the eggs to your liking and set aside.

Cut the buns in half and butter each side. Place a medium skillet on the stove over a medium heat. Put the bun tops and bottoms butter side down in the pan for a few seconds until lightly toasted. Remove the buns, and add 2–3 slices of beef to the bun bottoms, followed by 1–2 slices of Swiss cheese and 1 fried egg. Place the bun lid on top.

Serve immediately with yellow mustard and a dill pickle.

DEEP-FRIED AVOCADO TACOS

Unless you've spent the last few years in a permanent hungover fug, you can't help but notice that avocados are having a bit of a moment. But these stars of the healthy brunch scene have a darker, less virtuous secret—they taste amazing when deep-fried. Here the crispy-on-the-outside/creamy-soft-in-the-center avocado wedges are given the full taco treatment. Filthy.

2 avocados

1 cup/135g all-purpose/plain or self-raising flour mixed with 2 teaspoons baking powder

1 teaspoon ground avocado leaf powder or fennel seeds

2½ teaspoons ground cumin

4 teaspoons dried oregano

3 teaspoons paprika

½ teaspoon white pepper

½ teaspoon salt

11-fl. oz./330-ml bottle crisp lager

Vegetable oil, for frying

PICO DE GALLO

4 tomatoes, finely chopped

¼ onion, diced

¼ bunch of cilantro/coriander, finely chopped

¼ teaspoon salt

SERVE WITH

6 flour or corn tortillas, warmed (see page 4)

Herby slaw (see page 36) spiked with a dash of hot sauce

2 limes, each cut into 4 wedges

Thinly sliced radishes

MAKES 6

Cut the avocados in half, remove the stones, and peel off the skin. Cut each half lengthwise into 3–4 slices.

Put the flour in a large bowl. Add the avocado powder/fennel seeds, cumin, oregano, paprika, pepper, and salt, and mix together well. Make a well in the center, add the beer, and mix gently until you have a smooth batter.

Fill a small saucepan with vegetable oil to a depth of about 3 in./7.5 cm and place over a medium-high heat, or heat a deep-fat fryer to 350°F/180°C.

Meanwhile, to make the Pico de Gallo, place the ingredients in a bowl and mix well.

Coat the avocado slices in the batter, then carefully lower them into the hot oil and deep-fry for 30 seconds on each side until puffy and crisp, taking care not to burn them. Fry a few slices at a time.

Remove the slices from the oil with a slotted spoon and place on a plate lined with paper towels to absorb any excess oil.

To serve, layer up the tortillas with the avocado fritters, Pico de Gallo, slaw, and a squeeze of lime juice, and garnish with thinly sliced radishes. Serve with extra PDG and slaw.

ROASTED PO' BOYS

New Orleans, 12pm, the day after Mardi Gras. You're waking up groggy, covered in beads, after an epic night on Bourbon Street, where you drank lurid fluorescent cocktails until the sun came up. You need some Cajun cuisine to help soak up the booze so that you can rerun the fun this evening. These meat-free, plant-based po' boys should do the job nicely.

FOR THE EGGPLANT/ AUBERGINE

1 large eggplant/ aubergine, sliced into ½-in./1.5-cm thick rounds

Olive oil, for brushing

1–2 tablespoons Cajun spice mix

FOR THE WHITE BEAN PURÉE

1¼ cups/160 g canned white beans, drained and rinsed

1 tablespoon tahini

1 tablespoon fresh lemon juice

½ garlic clove, peeled

¼ teaspoon hot red pepper/dried chili flakes

¼ teaspoon smoked paprika

1–2 tablespoons ice-cold water (optional)

Salt, to taste

FOR THE HERBY SLAW

1 cup/60 g thinly sliced red cabbage

½ tightly packed cup/ 20 g fresh flat-leaf parsley or cilantro/ coriander leaves (or a mixture), finely chopped

½ garlic clove, finely grated

1 tablespoon olive oil

2 teaspoons apple cider vinegar

Sea salt, to taste

SERVE WITH

Fresh baguettes, cut into 6-in./15-cm lengths and split in half

Baking sheet, lined with parchment paper

MAKES 2-4

Preheat the oven to 400°F/200°C/ Gas 6.

Brush the eggplant/aubergine slices on both sides with oil and spread out on the prepared baking sheet. Sprinkle with a little of the Cajun spice mix to give a light coating.

Roast in the preheated oven for about 15 minutes. Flip the eggplant slices over and sprinkle the other side with Cajun spice mix. Bake for another 10 minutes, until soft and golden.

To make the white bean purée, combine all the ingredients in a food processor or blender and purée until smooth. Add the ice-cold water if you would like a smoother consistency.

Combine the slaw ingredients in a bowl and season to taste with salt.

Assemble the sandwiches with a good slathering of white bean purée on the baguettes, topped with the roasted eggplant slices and herby slaw.

③ COMFORT FOOD

DAMN HOT WINGS

Countless Jägerbombs battered your body into submission last night. Now you need a dish to shock your system back to life, like these ultra-hot wings. Be warned: they are not for the faint of heart.

Vegetable or canola oil, for frying

4 lb./1.8 kg chicken wings, halved at the joints, tips removed

1 stick/115 g butter

3 cups/750 ml hot sauce

2 tablespoons chopped fresh garlic

3 jalapeño peppers, deseeded and chopped

2 Thai chilis, deseeded and chopped

3 habanero peppers, deseeded and chopped

2 yellow wax peppers, deseeded and chopped

3 red chilis, deseeded and chopped

Salt and freshly ground black pepper

BLUE CHEESE SAUCE

1 cup/150 g crumbled blue cheese

¾ cup/150 g mayonnaise

½ cup/100 g sour cream

Deep-fat fryer

SERVES 4–6

Preheat the oil in a deep-fat fryer set to 350°F/180°C and preheat the oven to 400°F/200°C/Gas 6.

Fry the wings, 3–4 at a time, turning occasionally, until golden brown. Transfer to a shallow baking dish and bake in the preheated oven for 15 minutes, turning once, or until the juices run clear when the thickest part is pierced to the bone.

Melt the butter in a medium saucepan over a medium heat. Stir in the hot sauce, garlic, and peppers. Reduce the heat to medium-low and cook for 15 minutes, or until the peppers have softened. Season to taste with salt and pepper, then pour the sauce over the wings, turning to coat.

While the peppers are softening, make the Blue Cheese Sauce. Place all the ingredients in a medium bowl and whisk until combined.

Reduce the oven temperature to 350°F/180°C/Gas 4, return the wings to the oven, and bake for a further 10 minutes. Serve with the Blue Cheese Sauce.

SPAGHETTI AND MEATBALLS

In desperate hungover moments, many of us have succumbed and microwaved those meatballs festering in the freezer. The ones bought on a whim during an Ikea trip months (or was it years?) ago. Don't do that. Instead, cook this family recipe that's been passed down by generations of fuzzy-headed cooks. It's much tastier.

1 lb./500 g spaghetti

Salt, to taste

FOR THE SPAGHETTI SAUCE

¾ cup/90 g chopped onion

6 garlic cloves, minced

4 tablespoons extra-virgin olive oil

2 x 14-oz./400-g cans whole, peeled tomatoes

2 teaspoons sea salt

1 teaspoon granulated sugar

1 fresh bay leaf

6 oz./175 g tomato paste/purée

¾ teaspoon dried basil

½ teaspoon freshly ground black pepper

FOR THE MEATBALLS

2 tablespoons extra-virgin olive oil

½ lb./225 g lean ground/minced beef

½ lb./225 g ground thin/short rib

1 cup fresh breadcrumbs

1 tablespoon dried parsley

2 tablespoons grated Parmesan cheese

¼ teaspoon freshly ground black pepper

Pinch of garlic powder

1 egg, beaten

Freshly grated Parmesan cheese, to serve

SERVES 4

For the spaghetti sauce, in a large saucepan over a medium heat, sauté the onion and garlic in olive oil until the onion is translucent. Stir in the tomatoes, salt, sugar, and bay leaf. Cover the saucepan and reduce the heat to low. Simmer for 1–1½ hours. Stir in the tomato paste/purée, basil, and pepper. Refrigerate until ready to use.

Preheat the oven to 375°F/190°C/Gas 5.

For the meatballs, combine all the ingredients well in a mixing bowl with your hands and form into golf-ball size spheres. Place on a baking sheet and transfer to the preheated oven for 20 minutes. Use immediately or turn out onto a plate to cool and then place in the freezer.

Bring a pan of salted water to a boil and add the spaghetti. When it reaches an al dente texture, about 8–10 minutes, remove and drain. Mix with the sauce, add the meatballs, and finish by adding a generous sprinkling of freshly grated Parmesan cheese.

ROAST BEEF

It is true, there's a fair bit of work involved here, but nothing beats a proper roast for righting all wrongs and easing you into that contented place where a restorative nap in front of the TV feels like the perfect follow up.

6½ lb./3 kg bone-in forerib of beef (2–3 bones)

2 tablespoons all-purpose/plain flour

1 tablespoon hot mustard powder

3 oz./85 g beef dripping or shortening, or 4 tablespoons olive oil

3 onions, quartered

8–10 potatoes, cut into chunks and parboiled

5–6 parsnips, halved lengthwise

Sea salt and freshly ground black pepper

GRAVY

1 tablespoon fat from the pan

1 onion, thinly sliced

1 cup/250 ml beef stock

2 teaspoons cornstarch/cornflour, mixed with 2 teaspoons cold water

Sea salt and freshly ground black pepper

SERVE WITH

3 lb./1.25 kg vegetables, such as peas, carrots, or cabbage, sliced and steamed or boiled

Horseradish sauce

SERVES 8–10

Preheat the oven to 475°F/240°C/Gas 8. Season the meat to taste, mix the flour and mustard, and pat it onto the beef fat. Put the dripping or oil in a roasting pan, place the onions in the middle, and set the beef, fat side up, on top. Arrange the potatoes and parsnips around the meat and put the pan in the preheated oven.

After 20 minutes' cooking time, reduce the oven heat to 375°F/190°C/Gas 5, baste the beef, and turn the vegetables in the fat.

When the beef has been roasting for 1 hour 40 minutes, or when a meat thermometer registers 175°F/60°C (or a little below if you like beef very rare), take the beef out of the oven. Lift the beef onto a serving dish, add the vegetables, and set aside in a warm place. It will go on cooking as it rests.

For the gravy, put the roasting pan on top of the stove, heat the reserved 1 tablespoon of fat, add the onion, and cook slowly over a low heat until browned, about 30 minutes. Do not let burn. Add the stock and cornstarch/cornflour mixture, then season to taste with salt and pepper. Stir constantly over a low heat until the mixture boils, then simmer for a couple of minutes. Strain if you wish or serve as is. Pour into a gravy boat.

Meanwhile, cook your vegetables and place in a dish to keep warm. Put the beef on the table with the gravy and any extra sauces—horseradish is recommended.

CHICKEN POT PIE

Pie! That's just what's needed when you're feeling hungry yet fragile, and the flavors here are an absolute classic.

1½ cups/185 g all-purpose/plain flour

2 tablespoons/30 g butter

2 tablespoons sour cream

1 egg, lightly beaten

Sea salt and freshly ground black pepper

PIE FILLING

3 tablespoons/45 g butter

1½ lb./750 g chicken thigh fillets, cut into bite-size pieces

4 trimmed leeks, sliced

3 tablespoons all-purpose/plain flour

1 cup/250 ml chicken stock

½ cup/125 ml light/single cream

2 tablespoons chopped fresh tarragon

2 tablespoons roughly chopped fresh flat-leaf parsley

Your choice of vegetables, to serve

SERVES 4

To make the piecrust, mix the flour, butter, and a pinch of salt in a food processor for a few seconds. With the motor running, add the sour cream, half of the beaten egg, and 1–2 tablespoons of cold water, until the dough comes together. Roll into a ball, wrap in plastic wrap/clingfilm, and chill for 30 minutes.

Preheat the oven to 350°F/180°C/Gas 4. To make the filling, heat half of the butter in a skillet/frying pan over a high heat. When sizzling, brown the chicken for 2–3 minutes, turning often. Transfer to a bowl. Add the remaining butter to the skillet and cook the leeks over a medium heat for 2 minutes. Cover with a lid, reduce the heat, and cook for 2–3 minutes, until really softened.

Return the chicken to the pan and increase the heat to high. Sprinkle in the flour and cook for 2 minutes, stirring constantly so the flour thickly coats the chicken and leeks. Gradually add the stock, stirring all the time. Bring to a boil, then stir in the cream, tarragon, and parsley. Season well. Reduce the heat and simmer until thickened, about 1 minute. Remove from the heat and cool. Spoon into a pie dish.

Place the dough between 2 pieces of waxed/greaseproof paper and roll out to a thickness of ¼ in./5 mm, making sure the dough is more than big enough to cover the dish. Place the dough over the top of the pie, leaving the edges to overhang. Cut several slits in the top of the pie and gently press around the edges with a fork. Brush the remaining beaten egg over the top. Put the pie dish on a baking tray and cook in the preheated oven for 30 minutes, until the piecrust is golden.

Serve with your choice of veg—a heap of buttered new potatoes on the side is recommended.

SAUSAGES 'N' MASH

Who doesn't like a comforting plate of mash, piled with quality bangers and smothered with onion gravy? You? Get out of here!

8 good-quality sausages

ONION GRAVY

5 tablespoons/75 g unsalted butter, chilled and diced

2 onions, thinly sliced

1 garlic clove, crushed

1 tablespoon chopped fresh thyme

⅓ cup/80 ml ruby port (or red wine)

2 cups/500 ml beef stock

Sea salt and freshly ground black pepper

MASH

2 lb./900 kg potatoes, peeled and halved

3½ tablespoons/50 g butter

⅓ cup/80 ml milk

Wholegrain mustard

SERVES 3–4

For the gravy, melt 3 tablespoons/45 g of the butter in a saucepan and gently fry the onions, garlic, and thyme with a little seasoning for 15–20 minutes, or until soft and lightly golden. Add the port (or red wine), boil rapidly for 1 minute, then add the stock. Simmer for 10 minutes, or until reduced by half. Strain the sauce through a fine strainer and return to the pan. Reserve the onions. Simmer gently over a low heat and beat in the remaining butter a little at a time until the sauce is glossy. Return half the onions to the pan, heat, and serve hot.

Next, boil the potatoes in a large pan of salted water until soft and tender. This should take 15–20 minutes depending on the size of the potatoes. Drain the potatoes, return them to the pan along with the butter and milk, and mash until smooth. Season with salt and pepper, then stir through a tablespoon or two of wholegrain mustard to taste.

While the potatoes are cooking, broil/grill the sausages for 15 minutes until cooked, turning every few minutes.

To serve, put a good spoonful of mash onto each plate, add 2 or 3 sausages on top, and cover with onion gravy.

PIMENTO MAC 'N' CHEESE

It's hard to think of a meal more comforting than mac 'n' cheese. If this dish was a real person, it'd be rocking Ugg boots, a unicorn fleece onesie, and wrapped up in an enormous puffa jacket. Here, the comfort levels have been elevated further with the addition of pimento. If that's not enough, you could even chuck in leftover chicken wings, ham, or bacon for next-level contentment. Madness.

2 cups/240 g
dried macaroni

4 tablespoons/60 g butter

3 tablespoons all-purpose/
plain flour

1 teaspoon mustard powder

2¼ cups/530 ml milk

1¼ cups/115 g grated
mature Cheddar cheese

1¼ cups/115 g grated mild
Cheddar cheese

5 dashes of hot sauce

4-oz./115-g jar pimentos,
drained

Kosher/flaked salt

Freshly ground black pepper

SERVES 4–6

Preheat the oven to 350ºF/180ºC/Gas 4.

Fill a large saucepan with water, and bring to a rolling boil. Add 1 tablespoon of salt and the macaroni to the water. Cook for 5 minutes, then drain and set aside.

In the same saucepan, melt the butter over a medium heat. Add the flour, and whisk constantly for about 3 minutes, until the flour mixture is a light amber color. Add the mustard powder. Slowly whisk in the milk, and continue to whisk over a medium heat for about 5 minutes or until the sauce has thickened. Remove from the heat and add the grated cheeses and a few dashes of hot sauce, whisking until the cheese has melted. Season to taste with salt and pepper.

Return the macaroni to the saucepan with the cheese sauce and toss to coat. Stir in the drained pimentos.

Pour into a medium baking dish. Cover with foil and bake in the preheated oven for about 30 minutes, then remove the foil and bake for a further 10 minutes uncovered, until starting to brown on top and bubbling around the edges.

CHICKEN TIKKA MASALA

This homemade cuzza is much better than the takeaway crap you were drunkenly shoveling down your neck last night, direct from the foil container. For the full curry-house experience accompany it with a lager and follow it up by briefly microwaving a damp cloth from the bathroom to give your hands a wipe. Authentic!

4 boneless, skinless chicken breasts, cut into bite-size pieces

Salt and freshly ground black pepper

Cilantro/coriander leaves, chopped, and 1 red chili, sliced, to garnish

Naan or basmati rice, to serve

CHICKEN TIKKA MARINADE

1 cup/250 g plain yogurt

1 tablespoon fresh lemon juice

2 teaspoons ground cumin

1 teaspoon ground cinnamon

2 teaspoons cayenne pepper

2 teaspoons freshly ground black pepper

1 tablespoon grated ginger

TIKKA MASALA SAUCE

1 tablespoon/ 15 g butter

1 garlic clove, crushed

1 red chili (deseeded if desired), finely chopped

2 teaspoons ground cumin

3 teaspoons paprika

7-oz./200-g can chopped tomatoes

2 tablespoons tomato paste/purée

¾ cup/200 ml heavy/double cream

SERVES 4

To make the chicken tikka marinade, combine the yogurt, lemon juice, cumin, cinnamon, cayenne, black pepper, and ginger in a large glass bowl and season to taste with salt. Stir in the chicken, cover, and refrigerate for 4–6 hours or overnight.

Thread the marinated chicken onto metal skewers (discarding the marinade). Cook under a hot, preheated broiler/grill for about 5 minutes on each side.

Meanwhile, make the tikka masala sauce. Melt the butter in a large, heavy skillet/frying pan over a medium heat. Sauté the garlic and chili for 1 minute. Add the cumin and paprika, and season well.

Purée the tinned tomatoes in a blender until smooth, then add to the skillet with the tomato paste/purée and cream. Simmer over a low heat until the sauce has thickened, about 20 minutes.

Add the broiled chicken to the pan and simmer for 10 minutes, or until cooked through. Transfer to a serving platter and garnish with the cilantro/coriander and chili. Serve with warm naan or basmati rice.

RED LENTIL DAHL

Dahl is so hot right now! And that's not just down to the high levels of chili, its comforting qualities, or because it's vegan. Dahl earns top marks thanks to the fact it's easy to throw together, even at the pinnacle of your hangover—the point in the day when you're struggling to even string a sentence together. Lovely stuff.

Olive or coconut oil, for frying

2 onions, finely sliced

3 garlic cloves, minced

1-in./2.5-cm piece of fresh ginger, grated

2 teaspoons ground cumin

1 teaspoon ground turmeric

1 teaspoon ground coriander

½ teaspoon garam masala

¼ teaspoon cayenne pepper

14-oz./400-g can chopped tomatoes

1½ cups/270 g dried red lentils

2 carrots, finely diced

2 cups/120 g kale, shredded

Salt and freshly ground black pepper, to taste

SERVE WITH

Steamed rice

Pinch of hot red pepper/dried chili flakes

Freshly chopped cilantro/coriander

Coconut cream

SERVES 4–6

Heat enough oil to thinly coat the base of a large saucepan over a medium-high heat. Add the onions, season to taste with salt, and cook for about 10–12 minutes, stirring occasionally, until they begin to caramelize. Add a splash of water if the pan gets too dry.

Add the garlic and ginger and cook for another minute. Stir in the spices and cook for 1 more minute. Add the tomatoes and cook until bubbling again, then add 950 ml/ 4 cups of water and the lentils. Cover with a lid and bring to a boil.

Add the carrots, cover, and simmer for about 20–30 minutes until the lentils are starting to break down and the carrots are tender. Stir in some black pepper and the kale.

Turn off the heat, leave the pan covered, and let stand for 15 minutes before serving with rice, hot red pepper/dried chili flakes, cilantro/coriander, and a small drizzle of coconut cream.

SWEET POTATO FALAFEL

Falafel really are the best; a vegan treat even the most ardent meat eater enjoys—thanks to an association with late night visits to the kebab house. Make a batch in advance and reheat the next day.

2 medium-sized sweet potatoes (about 12 oz./ 350 g)

½ tightly packed cup/30 g cilantro/ coriander

⅓ tightly packed cup/25 g flat-leaf parsley leaves

2 large scallions/ spring onions, roughly chopped

3 garlic cloves, peeled

1 teaspoon ground cumin

1 teaspoon ground coriander

¼ teaspoon cayenne pepper

1 teaspoon baking powder

½ cup/60 g gram/ chickpea flour

Sesame seeds, to sprinkle (optional)

Salt, to taste

SERVE WITH

Diced cucumber

Diced tomato

Sliced red cabbage

Roughly chopped flat-leaf parsley

Juice of ½ lemon

Hummus

Pita breads

Salt and freshly ground black pepper

Baking sheet, greased with a thin layer of olive oil

MAKES 14–16 FALAFEL TO SERVE 4 PEOPLE

Preheat the oven to 425°F/220°C/Gas 7.

Poke the sweet potatoes with a fork a couple of times and roast for 40–60 minutes until soft. Remove from the oven and let cool. Once cooled, peel off and discard the skin.

Put the cilantro/coriander, parsley, scallions/ spring onions, and garlic in a food processor and pulse until everything is finely chopped. Alternatively, finely chop with a knife.

In a large bowl, mash the sweet potato flesh with a fork or masher until smooth. Season with salt, add the spices, baking powder, and gram/chickpea flour and stir quickly with a spatula or hand-held mixer until well combined. Stir in the herb, onion, and garlic mixture until evenly distributed. Let the dough rest in the fridge for 20 minutes.

Preheat the oven again to 400°F/200°C/ Gas 6. Scoop out portions of dough with a spoon and then lightly roll into golf-ball-size spheres using damp hands to prevent sticking. Put the falafel on the prepared baking sheet and sprinkle with sesame seeds, if using. Bake in the oven for 15–20 minutes until golden on the side touching the baking sheet.

To serve, combine some diced cucumber, tomato, sliced red cabbage, and parsley in a bowl with the fresh lemon juice and a little salt and pepper. Serve the falafel with the cucumber-cabbage salad and hummus, either in a bowl or packed into a pita bread.

BUTTERNUT SQUASH AND BLACK BEAN CHILLI

Anyone who's cooked a big pot of chilli knows that it always tastes better the next day. For that reason, this is a dream dish if you're planning a big night out. Add "making a chilli" to your pre-party prep and then smugly enjoy it 24 hours later while you're crusting on the sofa. Minimal hungover effort for maximum flavor. This version is vegan, but you can easily switch the butternut squash for beef.

Olive oil, for frying

1 onion, diced

3 cups/375 g peeled butternut squash, cut into ½-in./1.5-cm cubes

2 tablespoons tomato paste/purée

1 large garlic clove, minced

3 teaspoons ground cumin

2 teaspoons smoked paprika

¼ teaspoon ground cinnamon

¼ teaspoon cayenne pepper

14-oz./400-g can crushed or chopped tomatoes in juices

2 x 14-oz./400-g cans black beans in their liquid

Salt, to taste

SERVE WITH (OPTIONAL)

Diced avocado

Sour cream, vegan or regular

Chopped large scallions/spring onions

Corn chips

SERVES 4–6

In a large saucepan with a lid, heat enough oil to cover the base of the pan over a medium heat.

Add the onion, season to taste with salt, and cook for about 5 minutes until translucent. Add the butternut squash and cook, stirring occasionally, for 5 minutes.

Add the tomato paste/purée and stir. Cook for 1 minute. Add the garlic, cumin, paprika, cinnamon, and cayenne pepper, and cook for 1 minute more. Pour in the tomatoes and black beans along with the liquid from the cans. Season with salt and reduce the heat to medium-low.

Cook covered for about 30 minutes, stirring occasionally, until the butternut is tender. You may need to add ½ cup/125 ml or more of water, if the chilli becomes too dry or thick for your liking. Serve with your desired toppings.

VEGAN BURGERS

These days, the standard of vegan burgers is so high that they've been cocking a snook at the pallid pucks of gristle that constitute too many beef burgers out there. This smokily substantial plant-based patty is no exception and works with numerous top toppings.

Olive oil, for frying

1 small red onion, finely diced

2 garlic cloves, minced

2 tablespoons flaxseeds/
linseeds

½ cup/50 g rolled oats

2 x 14-oz./400-g cans black beans, drained and rinsed

2 medium beetroot, grated

2 tablespoons tomato paste/
purée

1½ teaspoons smoked paprika

1 teaspoon dried oregano

Salt and freshly ground
black pepper

SERVING SUGGESTIONS

Toasted buns

Barbecue sauce

Smashed avocado

Caramelized onions

Sliced tomato

Arugula/rocket or lettuce

Baking sheet, lined with
parchment paper

MAKES 6–8 PATTIES

Heat a thin layer of olive oil in a medium skillet/frying pan over a medium heat. Add the onion and cook, stirring, for about 5 minutes until softened. Add the garlic and cook for 1 minute more. Remove from the heat and set aside.

In a large bowl, combine the flaxseeds/linseeds with 6 tablespoons of water and let stand for 10 minutes.

Meanwhile, in a food processor, process the oats until they are finely chopped and bordering on a flour-like texture. Add the black beans to the food processor and pulse until they're finely chopped and combined with the oats, but not puréed.

Put the processed oats and black beans, grated beetroot, cooked onions and garlic, tomato paste/purée, smoked paprika, and oregano into the large bowl with the flaxseeds. Season to taste with salt and pepper, and mix with a rubber spatula or with your hands until everything is well combined. Form the mixture into 6–8 patties using damp hands, making them about 1 in./2.5 cm thick and about 3 in./7.5 cm wide.

In a large skillet, heat enough oil to cover the base over a medium-high heat. Add two patties and cook for 3–4 minutes on one side, until browned and firm. Flip and cook for another 3–4 minutes on the other side. Reduce the heat to medium if the patties are getting too charred. Remove and repeat with the remaining burgers.

Alternatively, you can lightly brush the burgers with oil and bake them on a baking sheet lined with parchment paper for 25 minutes in an oven preheated to 400°F/200°C/Gas 6, flipping them halfway through the cooking time.

Serve warm on toasted buns with your chosen toppings.

OREO PANCAKES

Just looking at these pancakes—packed with Oreos and doused in an epic chocolate sauce—runs the risk of you developing type-2 diabetes. But screw the guilt, in the state you're in they are so worth it.

PANCAKE BATTER

1¼ cups/160 g self-raising flour, sifted

1 teaspoon baking powder

1 egg, separated

1 teaspoon pure vanilla extract/vanilla bean paste

2 tablespoons caster/granulated sugar

Pinch of salt

1 cup/250 ml milk

2 tablespoons/30 g melted butter, plus extra for frying

9 Oreo cookies or similar, broken into pieces

CHOCOLATE FUDGE SAUCE

⅓ cup/30 g cocoa powder, sifted

1 teaspoon cold water

⅔ cup/150 ml heavy/double cream

3½ oz./100 g milk chocolate, chopped

1 tablespoon light corn syrup/golden syrup

1 tablespoon/15 g butter

Pinch of salt

1 teaspoon pure vanilla extract/vanilla bean paste

MAKES 12

To make the pancake batter, put the flour, baking powder, egg yolk, vanilla extract/vanilla bean paste, caster/granulated sugar, salt, and milk in a large mixing bowl and whisk together. Add the melted butter and whisk again. The batter should have a smooth, dropping consistency.

In a separate bowl, whisk the egg white to stiff peaks. Gently fold the whisked egg white into the batter mixture using a spatula Cover and put in the refrigerator to rest for 30 minutes.

For the chocolate fudge sauce, mix the cocoa powder with a little cold water until you have smooth paste. Put the cream, chocolate, cocoa paste, light corn syrup/golden syrup, butter, salt, and vanilla extract/vanilla bean paste in a saucepan or pot set over medium heat and simmer until the chocolate has melted and you have a smooth, glossy sauce. Keep the pan on the heat but turn it down to low to keep the sauce warm until you are ready to serve.

When you are ready to serve, remove your batter mixture from the refrigerator and stir once. Put a little butter in a large skillet/frying pan set over a medium heat. Let the butter melt and coat the base of the pan, then ladle small amounts of the batter into the pan. Sprinkle some of the Oreo cookies into the batter and cook until the batter is just set, then turn over and cook for a further 2–3 minutes. Once cooked, keep the pancakes warm while you cook the remaining batter in the same way, adding a little butter to the pan each time, if required.

Serve the pancakes in a stack with the hot chocolate fudge sauce poured over the top.

VEGAN GOOEY CHOCOLATE COOKIES

As a counterpoint to the explosion of sugar outlined in the last recipe, these vegan cookies are full of cocoa flavor and not overly sweet, satisfying your chocolate craving the second you take a first bite. Definitely one for the more sophisticated hangover sufferer.

2¼ oz./60 g bittersweet/dark vegan chocolate, broken into pieces

⅓ cup/65 ml sunflower oil

⅓ cup/75 ml soy(a) milk

¾ cup/200 g rice, maple, or agave syrup

¼ teaspoon bourbon vanilla powder

1 cup/125 g unbleached all-purpose/plain flour

2 tablespoons cocoa powder

¾ teaspoon baking powder (ideally aluminum-free)

¼ teaspoon sea salt

¼ teaspoon ground cinnamon

Baking sheet, lined with parchment paper

MAKES ABOUT 24 COOKIES

Melt the chocolate in a heatproof bowl set over a pan of barely simmering water. Take care not to let the underside of the bowl touch the surface of the water. In a large mixing bowl, whisk the oil, milk, syrup, and vanilla powder. Add the melted chocolate. Preheat the oven to 350°F/180°C/Gas 4. Place a strainer/sieve over the bowl containing the liquid ingredients (this way you won't need to use two separate bowls).

Put the flour, cocoa powder, baking powder, salt, and cinnamon directly in the strainer and sift everything until it passes through the net. Use a spatula to incorporate all the ingredients into a smooth batter. It should not slide down the spoon—if it does, chill the batter in the fridge for 10 minutes.

Line a baking sheet with parchment paper and, using a tablespoon, drop the batter onto it, ½ in./1 cm apart. Bake for 12–14 minutes. The dough is dark to start with, so it's easy to burn the cookies, and you want them still soft to the touch when you remove them from the oven. So check for doneness after 12 minutes, and bake them for no longer than 14 minutes.

Remove from the oven, slip the baking sheet with cookies onto the countertop or a cold tray, and let cool. Store in a cookie jar for a week or so.

BANANA BREAD FRENCH TOAST

An evening of decadent French wine necessitates a morning of indulgent French toast to clear the cobwebs. The *pièce de résistance* here is the use of banana bread to add a certain *je ne sais quoi*, but stick to regular bread if you want *la vie en rose*. Slather in maple syrup, or any other sweet sauce for that matter. *Bon appétit*!

BANANA BREAD

2 cups/280 g all-purpose/plain flour

1 teaspoon baking powder

¼ teaspoon salt

1 stick/115 g butter, plus extra for greasing

¾ cup/150 g brown sugar

2 eggs, beaten

5 ripe bananas, mashed

FRENCH TOAST

3 eggs

3 tablespoons sweetened condensed milk

1 teaspoon pure vanilla extract/ vanilla bean paste

2 tablespoons/ 30 g butter

1 loaf banana bread (see above)

Confectioners'/icing sugar, for dusting

Maple syrup, to serve

Loaf pan (9 x 5 in./ 23 x 13 cm), lightly greased

SERVES 4

Preheat the oven to 350°F/180°C/Gas 4. Grease the loaf pan.

To make the banana bread, in a large bowl, combine the flour, baking powder, and salt. In a separate medium bowl, cream together the butter and brown sugar. Stir the eggs in one at a time and add the mashed bananas until combined. Add the banana mixture to the flour mixture and stir with a wooden spoon until mixed together. Pour into the greased loaf pan. Bake for 1 hour, or until a toothpick/cocktail stick inserted into the center comes out clean. Let cool for 5–10 minutes and then turn it out onto a wire rack.

To make the French toast, in a small-medium bowl, beat the eggs, sweetened condensed milk, and vanilla with a fork. Set aside.

Melt the butter in a large skillet/frying pan over a medium heat. Cut the banana bread into 4 thick slices. Dip each slice into the egg mixture and place in the hot skillet. Cook on each side for 1–2 minutes until golden brown. Plate and dust with confectioners'/icing sugar. Serve with a side of maple syrup.

MIRACLE PANCAKES

A hangover miracle meal that's nutritious AND delicious? We've got to be yanking your crank! Rejoice, non-believer, because it's true—these divine pancakes genuinely are full of healthy fats, antioxidants, and fiber to help you atone for the previous evening's sins. Hallelujah!

Generous ⅓ cup/50 g potato starch

½ teaspoon baking/bicarbonate of soda

1½ teaspoons baking powder

½ cup/70 g buckwheat flour

Scant ½ cup/60 g brown rice flour

3 tablespoons milled flaxseeds/linseeds

½ teaspoon sea salt

1 teaspoon ground cinnamon

2 cups/480 ml almond milk

2 eggs (see note)

1 teaspoon vanilla extract

Vegetable oil, for frying

SERVE WITH

Maple syrup, to taste

Handful of blueberries, (optional)

SERVES 2–4

Sift the potato starch, baking/bicarbonate of soda, and baking powder into a mixing bowl. Add the remaining dry ingredients and set aside. In another bowl, combine the almond milk, eggs, and vanilla extract. Add the wet to the dry ingredients slowly and whisk to make a thick batter.

Heat a little oil in a large skillet/frying pan over a medium-high heat. Drop the batter from a spoon into the pan to form six round circles. Cook until small bubbles form on the top of each pancake. Flip and cook for a further 3 minutes or until golden brown in color.

Serve the pancakes immediately, stacked on a plate and drizzled with maple syrup. Blueberries make a tasty addition, if desired, and are a powerful antioxidant.

NOTE: If you prefer not to eat eggs, use egg replacer or make a flax-egg mix by combining 2 tablespoons of ground flaxseeds/linseeds with 6 tablespoons of water.

STICKY TOFFEE PUDDING

Sticky toffee pudding is an insanely good dessert and an absolute must-inhale when you're feeling at your lowest ebb. This recipe is a good, simple introduction to this king of desserts, which is exactly as it should be for a book on hangovers. It suggests serving with cream or vanilla ice cream, but how about a gallon of custard instead? Go on, devour in seconds and then get your tongue in there to lick the bowl clean. You know you want to.

⅓ cup/75 ml dulce de leche

1 stick/115 g unsalted butter, at room temperature

⅔ cup/115 g sugar

2 eggs

¾ cup/115 g self-raising flour

¼ cup/40 g walnut pieces

Heavy (double) cream or vanilla ice cream, to serve

6 pudding molds or 1 pudding basin

SERVES 6

Pour or spoon the dulce de leche into the bottom of 6 individual buttered pudding molds or a buttered pudding basin.

Beat together the butter and sugar until pale and creamy, then beat in the eggs, one at a time. Sift over the flour and fold in, then stir in the walnuts. Pour the mixture into the molds or basin.

Cover each pudding with 2 sheets of foil and tie firmly in place with a piece of kitchen string.

Put the puddings in a large pan and pour boiling water into the pan about two-thirds of the way up the sides of the puddings. Cover with a lid and simmer gently for about 1½ hours, checking the water level occasionally and topping up if necessary.

To serve, remove the foil, invert the pudding(s) onto serving plate(s), and lift off. Serve warm with heavy/double cream or ice cream.

INDEX

RECIPE CREDITS

SUSANNAH BLAKE: Eggs Florentine 11; Sticky Toffee Pudding 62

ROSS DOBSON: Chicken Pot Pie 42

DOG 'N' BONE BOOKS: Sausage 'n' Mash 43

AMY RUTH FINEGOLD: Miracle Pancakes 61

FELIPE FUENTES CRUZ & BEN FORDHAM: Ham and Eggs Tacos 6; Burger Tacos 22; Deep-fried Avocado Tacos 34

DUNJA GULIN: Tofu Scramble 17; Vegan Gooey Chocolate Cookies 58

CAROL HILKER: Steak and Egg Skillet 8; Paris-style Eggs Benedict 10; Belgian Waffle with Maple Bacon 12; Fish Finger Sandwich 20; Ultimate Grilled Cheese Sandwich 24; Pastrami Reuben 26; Club Sandwich 28; Steak Sandwich 30; Salt Beef Hash Egg Sandwich 32; Damn Hot Wings 38; Spaghetti and Meatballs 40; Pimento Mac 'n' Cheese 44; Banana Bread French Toast 60

DAN MAY: Huevos Rancheros 6

HANNAH MILES: Oreo Pancakes 56

SHELAGH RYAN: Sausage and Egg Muffins 14; Chorizo Mushroom Eggs 16

SONIA STEVENSON: Roast Beef 41

LEAH VANDERVELDT: Roasted Po' Boys 36; Red Lentil Dahl 48; Sweet Potato Falafel Kebabs 50; Butternut Squash And Black Bean Chilli 52; Vegan Burgers 54

SUNIL VIJAYAKAR: Chicken Tikka Masala 46